LAWS AND SAUSAGE

LAWS AND SAUSAGE

YOU NEVER WANT TO SEE EITHER ONE GET MADE!

Tips and tricks on how *anyone* can influence the public policy process!

Brian S. Trascher

Foreword by
Retired Congressman Bob Livingston (R-LA)

L&S PUBLISHING

A division of Laws and Sausage, LLC

New Orleans, LA

COPYRIGHT © 2017
ALL RIGHTS RESERVED

Published in 2017 by L&S Publishing

All rights reserved. No part of this publication may be reproduced or transmitted in any form or by any means electronic or mechanical, including photocopying, recording, scanning, digitizing, or any information storage and referral system, without written permission from the publisher. Requests for permission to make copies of any part of this book should be sent to:

Laws and Sausage, LLC
141 Robert E. Lee Blvd. #308
New Orleans, LA 70124
www.lawsandsausage.net

Copyright © 2017 by L&S Publishing,
A division of Laws and Sausage, LLC.

Library of Congress Card Number: 2017901587
Main entry under title: Laws and Sausage

ISBN: 978-0692840610

Authored by Brian S. Trascher
Cover and Book Design by Brian S. Trascher and Eunice Roland

Printed in the United States of America

For my beautiful princess Vivian. You are my eyes, my heart, my soul, and my everything.

-Daddy

TABLE OF CONTENTS

Foreword vii

Preface viii

Acknowledgements xii

Chapter 1: Do lobbyists live in the lobby? 1

Chapter 2: Am I a lobbyist, an advocate, or an activist? 8

Chapter 3 : How do I start the policy making process? 15

Chapter 4: Is my issue local, state, or federal? 22

Chapter 5: How can I create awareness for my issue? 33

Chapter 6: How important is the timing of my campaign? 41

Chapter 7: When and how do I schedule my first meeting? 48

Chapter 8: My meeting is set, now what? 55

Chapter 9: It's meeting day, am I ready? 63

Chapter 10: What do I do after my meetings? 69

Chapter 11: Is this really how my government works? 85

Resources 95

Index 100

FOREWORD

Despite public perception, "lobbyist" is not equated with a four-letter word. Lobbying is as honorable a profession as is the practice of law, medicine, or engineering. There is good and bad in any profession, and that's certainly true among lobbyists. But just as you wouldn't want your lawyer in charge of removing your gallbladder, neither should you want just anyone navigating your interests through a myriad of legislative and regulatory processes. Significant political experience makes the difference between success and failure.

"Laws & Sausage" is an eminently readable and concise explanation of the importance of a lobbyist. It is an entertaining and informative description of the role and tools available to be an effective practitioner. Laws and regulations governing lobbying are demanding. Honesty, integrity and rigid adherence to the rules are imperative to a successful lobbying career. Without them, a lobbyist stands to risk reputation, clients, and even investigation and/or public sanction.

Brian Trascher has learned well his profession as a lobbyist. His work serves as an indispensable primer for prospective clients, lobbyists and political junkies of all stripes.

Bob Livingston
Member of Congress (Retired)
President, The Livingston Group

PREFACE

On March 29, 1869, The Daily Cleveland Herald quoted poet John Godfrey Saxe as saying, "Laws, like sausages, cease to inspire respect in proportion as we know how they are made." Even before the days of big money Super PAC's, fancy television ads, and cable news, Saxe perfectly captured the truth about the American political process. If you've never seen sausage being made, you ought to watch a video of the process. It's possible that you'll never eat another link of sausage again. The same can be said about how laws are made. If most ordinary people got to see how the American legislative process really worked, they may become so jaded that they would never want to vote again.

Most people know what is being referred to when someone references "the world's oldest profession." It is often said that politics is the second oldest profession, and that it's ironic how closely it resembles the first. All cynicism aside, most Americans who seek public office do so out of a sense of duty, service, and a desire to change their community and country for the better. Like in any profession, however, there have always been a handful of bad apples that gave the rest a bad name. But because scandals and mistakes sell more newspapers and advertising, the successes and victories of the public policy process rarely get reported to the American people.

It's very common for the United States of America to be referred to as a democracy. In a democracy, voters determine everything from their leaders to national policy. Since it would be impractical to hold a referendum for each of the millions of pieces of legislation that move at the federal, state, and local level every year, we elect representatives who serve as trustees to make those decisions for us. Therefore, we are really a democratic republic.

Because we are governed by aldermen, city councilmen, mayors, county commissioners, state legislators, governors, congressmen, and presidents, there comes with it a very large and complex public policy process. This process involves many steps.
It usually starts with an idea, then it is drafted into legislation, then follows procedural and committee hurdles, then goes through multiple votes – sometimes in multiple bodies, then goes for executive consent, and sometimes can face a judicial challenge. Still, in between these steps that can vary depending on jurisdiction, there are often public hearings and media scrutiny that can have just as much or more of an effect than the official public policy process itself.

It is generally considered a landslide victory when a substantive piece of legislation becomes law on its first attempt. While laws can generally be passed quickly at the local level, the average time it takes for a new piece of legislation to pass at the state level is three years, and seven years at the congressional level. This glacial pace of activity is generally to blame for the low approval ratings of the U.S. Congress, but it also has as much to do with partisan gridlock. In any case, for nearly every piece of legislation introduced at every level of government, there are usually interested parties who either support or oppose it. That's where government relations professionals, or "lobbyists" come in to play.

Lobbyists represent different organizations covering a wide variety of issues in exchange for compensation. They come from different backgrounds, but the common denominator is that they all have experience navigating the public policy process, as well as the contacts and relationships to effectuate results. This book will go into the many ways that the process and the officials who control it can be influenced, and *Laws and Sausage* is meant to serve as a guide for anyone who seeks to achieve results from their government regardless of their experience or education.

Most large corporations, trade organizations, and special interest groups hire professional lobbyists to manage their policy agendas. While this is a necessary tactic to ensure the best results, most of them don't think to double up on their efforts by utilizing their rank and file industry officials, executives, and employees.

The truth is that anyone can learn to effectively communicate with their elected officials. In fact, there are many cases in which a grassroots effort bears more fruit than a professional political strategy. But even in large scale operations, grassroots are a powerful supplement to any campaign. There is virtually no industry in America that isn't regulated by some governmental body or agency. Therefore, no matter what you do for a living, these entities can affect your life in ways you might not even realize. It is worth your time to learn how you can assist your industry by engaging the very policymakers who make these impactful decisions.

In addition to being a registered lobbyist, Brian Trascher gives keynote speeches and workshops around the country showing these organizations how to use their existing workforces to help move their industry's issues and agendas through the maze of the legislative process. For more information on how to bring *Laws and Sausage* into your organization, visit

www.lawsandsausage.net.

ACKNOWLEDGEMENTS

Down in Louisiana, they say every young man catches politics like a disease. I was no exception to this rule. It's hard to pinpoint the exact genesis of my infatuation with the political world, because no one in my family had run for political office or been involved in any political campaigns that I am aware of. I know that my parents watched the news and voted, but aside from that they were not very politically active.

Although I was born during the Ford administration, Ronald Reagan was the first president that I have early childhood memories of. Even though I was only 5 years old in 1980, I can distinctly remember watching the Reagan-Carter debate (my parents must have been watching it) when Ronald Reagan gave his famous come back, "There you go again!" to Jimmy Carter. I knew absolutely nothing about politics yet, but at that moment I had a gut feeling that Reagan would win the election.

When I was in high school, I read a story about a young man who had been elected to congress at the age of 25. I remember thinking to myself, "Wow, he's only eight years older than me and he is already a congressman!" After reading the constitution, I also learned that 25 was the minimum age for someone to be eligible to run for congress, so this guy must have started preparing early.

When I was a senior in high school, civics was probably the only class that I never fell asleep in. My teacher, Ricky Nuesslein, was different than all the others I had. While going through the subject matter, he would often go off on tangents adding in his personal opinions on different political issues. Usually it was about all the ways the government pissed him off. He was hilarious.

One day, Mr. Nuesslein invited the congressman from Louisiana's 1st district to address all of the seniors. At the time, the seat was held by long-time Republican Congressman Bob Livingston. Livingston had been in office since 1976 and served until 1998, and for the last few years he chaired the powerful House Appropriations Committee. He was in line to become Speaker, but left Congress to start his own lobbying firm. He gave us an "inside baseball" view of what it was like to be a congressman, and I instantly became a fan. To this day, Bob graciously takes time out of his busy schedule to visit with my business partner and I when we are on the hill. This is a man who saw the sausage maker from the inside for over two decades, so his advice and guidance has been invaluable to our success in the business.

That year in particular was when Bill Clinton challenged George H.W. Bush for the presidency. In watching the distinct contrast between the ideologies of the two candidates, I started to realize that my own political views were more conservative. I remember thinking at the time that Mr. Nuesslein was likely a Republican, but looking back he was probably more of a Libertarian. He railed against most types of government intervention and rarely had anything good to say about any politicians on either side of the aisle. At age 41, I still have the attention span of a gnat, but Ricky Nuesslein managed to keep my attention for an hour a day when I was only 17. I have no doubt that his special brand of teaching planted some early seeds in what would ultimately become my career.

I went to college at Louisiana State University in Baton Rouge. Being in the capital city meant I was surrounded by the political hub of Louisiana government, which easily has one of the most colorful histories in America. It is said that Louisiana voters don't tolerate corruption, they demand it.

In 1996, one of my professors told me about an essay contest where the winners would be selected as youth delegates to the Republican National Convention in San Diego, California. Apparently, he thought I was a decent enough writer and encouraged me to send in an essay.

I ended up being one of four youth delegates selected from Louisiana. The only catch was that I had to cover my own airfare as well as a program fee, which all ended up being around $700.00. My parents were nice enough to pick up the tab, they figured the networking could lead me to a political job. They were right.

After the convention, I went to work for the Bob Dole campaign organizing volunteers on college campuses. Bill Clinton's staff was able to suppress the Monica Lewinsky story until after the election (probably the inspiration for the movie *Wag the Dog*), so he won re-election comfortably. The experience taught me a lot about the nuts and bolts of campaigning, and I was hooked for life.

After the election, I went to work for a pro-charter school organization back in Louisiana. I had never lobbied the legislature before, but at that point I knew my way around the capital well enough to fake it. I was able to work closely with the governor's staff on many pieces of education policy, and eventually I was offered a job in the governor's press office.

Although I wasn't directly involved in legislative affairs, being in the press office put me on the pulse of everything going on in the administration. The press secretary was an eccentric but brilliant woman. She was an absolute beast at handling the media, probably because she has been a journalist for many years prior to working for the administration. It was there that I learned invaluable skills in political communications and media relations. These skills are something that many lobbyists never learn, but all should have in order to be successful in this industry. I still keep up with that press secretary to this day, and she is ornerier than ever. But I love her just the same and will always be grateful for her mentorship.

After leaving the governor's office, I had a few stints in corporate government affairs over a decade or so. In 2009, I finally set up my own shop with a partner and we have never looked back. Our firm, Gulf South Strategies, represents clients in multiple states. We lobby every level of government from municipalities, state legislatures, and congress.

Public speaking has always played a big role in my career, but it wasn't until I met speaking coach Steve Siebold that I learned how to turn it into another income stream. Steve and his wife Dawn gave me the guidance and inspiration to learn to speak like a pro, write this book, and create the *Laws and Sausage* workshop.

Finally, I wouldn't be anywhere close to where I am today without the love and support of my entire family. I am eternally grateful for their tolerance.

LAWS AND SAUSAGE

"Modern politics are like professional wrestling. The battles are scripted and the outcomes are usually predetermined. The key is to be in the room while the script is being written."

-Brian S. Trascher

Laws and Sausage
You never want to see either one get made!

CHAPTER ONE

DO LOBBYISTS LIVE IN THE LOBBY?

When people ask if governmental relations professionals are referred to as "lobbyists" because they spend all their time in the lobby, I always answer the same way: Bad lobbyists wait in the lobby, good lobbyists use a different door.

But the number one question I get asked is "What does a lobbyist do?" It's pretty simple, we legally and ethically influence politicians to do what we want them to do. Actually, we get them to do what the people who are paying us want them to do. It's said that he who represents himself has a fool for a client. This saying originally referred to representing yourself before a judge, but applies appropriately to representing yourself in front of a governmental or regulatory body. In fact, without the legislative branch of government, the courts would have no laws to interpret and little need for lawyers.

Whether you're looking at it from the bottom up or top down, government is very similar to the interstate highway system. There are straight lines, curvy lines, entrances and exits, traffic, road blocks, and sometimes construction. Depending on what your issue is, navigating these roads by yourself can be a very daunting task. Imagine taking a road trip to a place you've never been before. A seasoned lobbyist is someone who has an up to date GPS system. My hope is that after reading this book, you'll at the very least have an up to date fold out map.

If you read the preface of this book, you'll remember when I said that there are very few industries that are not regulated by some government entity. Therefore, there are scores of elected officials, political appointees, and bureaucrats who make daily decisions that can affect your job and your livelihood. It was one of the world's first mayors, Pericles of Athens (430 B.C.) who said, "Just because you don't take an interest in politics doesn't mean that politics won't take an interest in you."

In election years, we hear from all sorts of people who tell us how important is to exercise our right to vote. They even sometimes try to guilt us into voting by pointing out how many people on earth don't have that right, or reminding us of how many people died before us so that we would continue to have that right. Even if you're not a political junkie like me, you might still vote because you know someone who is on the ballot, because of a particular issue or set of issues you feel strongly about, or perhaps just out of a sense of civic duty. All of those reasons are fine, but should we really be so quick to shame people who choose not to vote? Let me put it another way, do you really want people who don't pay at least a *little* bit of attention to the issues or the candidates voting? Should low information voters have as much of a voice in an election as those who take the time to educate themselves on current events? Of course, if those folks are eligible to vote then they have every right to do so, but should we encourage them to?

This may sound rather cynical, and it is in no way a suggestion that any eligible voter should be disenfranchised for any reason. But if an eligible voter can't find some sense of having skin in the game within any given election, then they are probably doing the rest of us a favor by staying home. Most laws that get passed are done so with good intentions, but two of the most common words you will hear in the halls of government are "unintended consequences." This refers to the moment that policy makers realize that a law has caused some type of inefficiency or inconvenience that was not anticipated beforehand.

In case you are wondering why the percentage of people who don't vote keeps going up, it's because of something called the "motor voter" law. The motor voter law was designed to get more people on the voter rolls by automatically registering them when they obtain or renew a driver's license. It achieved the objective of adding more voters to the rolls, but it also turned a lot unregistered non-voters into registered non-voters, thus driving up the statistical percentage of Americans who don't vote. My point in telling you all of this is threefold. First, when we get to the section of the book that deals with crafting legislation, it's important to be careful what you wish for, because unintended consequences come up more than you might think. Second, if you want to play the political game, it's important to be both educated on your issue as well as willing to vote on it. Third, as you'll see later in this book when we go over setting up a meeting with an elected official, you'll learn why your credibility can be initially judged by your track record of participation in the political process.

Hopefully you now have a basic understanding of what a lobbyist does. If you have the budget and your issue or issues are complex enough, it would be wise to hire a professional to represent you.

When the issues are large and affect a wide range of people, it usually means that either a new or existing organization can be relied on to raise funds and help provide the resource materials your lobbyist will need during the campaign. But if your issue is less complex, or you just don't have the budget for a lobbyist and you're forced to go it alone, then *Laws and Sausage* will provide the tips and tricks needed to help you take the system head-on like a professional.

In the ensuing chapters of this book, we'll go over what you need to know to get started:

- Building your network of allies both inside and outside of government
- Taking the political temperature with regards to your issue
- Determining the body of jurisdiction (city, county, state, federal)
- Identifying your sponsor
- Diagnosing the process of passage
- Targeting key staffers
- Setting your meeting with policy makers
- Preemptively dealing with possible amendments and compromise
- Preparing public testimony
- Tracking your legislation
- Anticipating legal challenges
- Knowing when, and when not to take a victory lap

And these are just the highlights! You might feel like you're drinking from a firehose right now, but fear not, the first step to swimming across the English Channel is jumping off the pier.

Remember, you're just getting started in this racket. Just like the slow-moving wheels of justice, the business of government is in no more a hurry than a sunbathing crocodile.

"When buying and selling is controlled by legislation, the first thing to be bought and sold are legislators."

-P.J. O'Rourke

Laws and Sausage
You never want to see either one get made!

CHAPTER TWO

AM I A LOBBYIST, AN ADVOCATE, OR AN ACTIVIST?

Every citizen of the United States has a right to petition the government, and that right extends to interacting with their elected officials and even non-elected policy makers within the government. Let's say that you are having a problem with the Internal Revenue Service. You can contact your local congressman or one of the two US Senators from your state, and ask that they write a letter requesting assistance for you with the Taxpayer Advocacy Program (this is a program within the IRS that works with people having tax problems.) This does not make you a lobbyist, an advocate, or an activist.

If you contact a member of Congress about the IRS on behalf of someone else but are not paid for doing so, then you could technically be called an advocate. Let's say that your experience with the IRS leads you to recognize some ongoing problems that are affecting many people like yourself, and you have some ideas on reforms that could be implemented to avoid these types of problems in the future. You then start to contact members of Congress to pitch your ideas and garner support for legislation or regulatory changes that achieve your goals. If you're not being paid by anyone and you aren't spending money entertaining these policy makers, then you are more than likely an advocate. These are not exactly "hard and fast" rules, but are just examples to lay some groundwork that will help you distinguish between the three.

Now, when and if you start to receive compensation, or if you make any expenditures in your efforts that include gifts or entertainment for the people you are trying to influence, then you start to cross into the waters of being considered a lobbyist. Notice that I said "receive compensation *or* make expenditures" during the course of your efforts. This is because in most cases, you don't have to do both in order to be considered a lobbyist. Many state ethics laws, including federal, say that spending money on those you mean to influence, even you are not personally being paid to do so, technically makes you a lobbyist. Even if you are using your own money to make these expenditures and not being reimbursed for them by anyone, most ethics laws say that your actions technically constitute lobbying, and deem that the expenditures must be reported.

Every state and the federal government has their own ethics rules which govern interactions between elected officials and those they serve. Depending on whether you plan to do your work locally or at the state level, you should consult that state's ethics laws to see what parameters your activities may fall under, if any. If you plan to work at the federal level, you will need to refer to the Lobbyist Disclosure Act of 2008. A copy of the rules can be found at www.senate.gov/LDA.

By definition, a lobbyist is generally considered as a person who attempts to influence a policy maker in exchange for compensation. As explained above, you can also be considered a lobbyist if you make expenditures on a policy maker. Some ethics laws are very straightforward, some are very complicated, and some (in my opinion) come very close to violating the 1st Amendment of the constitution. But that is another argument for another day. In any case, many of these laws were created or tightened up as a result of the Jack Abramoff lobbying scandal of 2005. If you aren't familiar with it, the short version of the story is that a group of lobbyists, led by Abramoff, were accused and convicted of paying off high ranking members of Congress in cash, trips, and lavish gifts. It was a gross perversion of what legitimate governmental relations professionals are supposed to be, and thus many restrictions on lobbyist activities were enacted.

Most of these ethics laws deal more with expenditures by lobbyists than the compensation they receive. I'm not aware of any laws that limit the amount of compensation that a lobbyist can receive, but most of them place limits on how much can be spent on policy makers for gifts and entertainment. There are also certain types of government employees, particularly staff members, that lobbyists are prohibited from spending any money on. Once you fit the definition of a lobbyist, you are usually required to register with whichever ethics department has jurisdiction over the governmental entity or entities you intend to lobby. This registration can generally be done online and in most cases, involve registration fees. Ironically, there are no rules limiting how much the government can charge a lobbyist for his or her registration fees. Just like in Las Vegas, the house always wins.

So, what happens if you work for a company or organization in which at least part of your job duties include interacting with policy makers? It depends. In most cases, you can talk to policy makers on behalf of your employer without registering as a lobbyist if that type of activity constitutes a minimal amount of your average work week. Every state is different, but a good rule of thumb is that as long as you aren't spending more than 20% of your typical work week interacting with policy makers, then you probably won't have to register as a lobbyist even though you are receiving a salary from your employer. However, if within that 20% of activity you make any expenditures on those policy makers, then you may very well be required to register. If you avoid breaching these barriers, then you can just be considered an advocate. In my experience, most employers who have employees meet with policy makers regularly will let them register as lobbyists just to avoid any potential of violating ethics rules. This is what I would recommend as best practices.

Many non-profit organizations are prohibited from lobbying activities in order to keep their non-profit status. However, many of these organizations receive public funding and deal with regulatory agencies on a frequent basis, so it's in their best interest to stay close to policy makers and up to date on changes that affect their operations. For this reason, they can take advantage of a loophole that allows them to hire people who act as "community educators", whose job it is to promote the awareness of the mission of their organization as well as their successes. These employees or contractors may also educate policy makers as well, but are still bound by the same ethics rules as everyone else. So just because your employer may call you an "advocate", refer to the information in this chapter when determining if you should register as a lobbyist.

Activists are defined as people who campaign for some type of social change. They are usually involved in protests and public demonstrations in support or opposition to an issue. They generally don't meet one on one with policy makers, but if you fit the definition of an activist, then you should also refer to the information in this chapter to determine if you should register as a lobbyist.

"Just because you don't take an interest in politics doesn't mean politics won't take an interest in you."

-Pericles (430 B.C.)

CHAPTER THREE

HOW DO I START THE POLICY MAKING PROCESS?

As mentioned in the preface of this book, politics is considered the second oldest profession in the world. But as long as there has been politics, there have been people trying to influence politicians for their own or for a third party's benefit. I guess that ranks lobbying somewhere between the second and third oldest profession.

But like anything old, the lobbying industry has been very resistant to change. Most lobbyists were trained by other lobbyists, or they paid close attention to the ones that came before them, so the traditional mechanics of the business have remained largely the same for a very long time. Sure, technology has changed the way we operate a good bit. Most governmental entities have websites, you can track most legislation online, e-mail and text messaging has become more of a mainstream way to communicate with elected officials, and conversely, electronic messaging and social media have become the new normal for policy makers to communicate with their constituents. But the boots on the ground process of passing and killing legislation has not evolved too much past the guy second from the left on the evolutionary chart.

When I was a kid and my mother used to cook pot roast, she would cut the roast in half and put each half into two pots. I never understood why she did this, so one day I decided to ask. She told me that it was the way her mother cooked pot roast, so that's the way she learned it. So, I asked my grandmother the same question and she gave me the same answer, she learned the pot roast cooking technique from her mother. Still curious, and aided by the fact that my great-grandmother was still alive, I asked her if she cooked pot roast in one pot or two. She told me that she just used one pot. When I told her that my mom and grandmother said that the two-pot system had been passed down from her, she said, "Oh yeah, I did it that way a long time ago, but not anymore." So naturally I asked her why she was down to one pot, and she looked at me like I had grown another head and said, "Well, because your great-grandfather bought me a bigger pot."

Whether you are a lobbyist, an advocate, or an activist, never accept that you must do what everyone else is doing just because that's the way it's always been done. Policy makers talk to countless numbers of people every day, and regardless of their issues, almost all of them sound the same. The first thing you need to do to make a lasting impression is stand out from the crowd.

So here you are. You're engaged and informed, you watch the news, you vote, you go to your neighborhood association meetings, you go to town hall meetings, and you know who your elected officials are (you should, because they work for you.) Then suddenly, an issue comes up that affects your life. It's a proposed ordinance, law, or regulation that is going to adversely affect you. Or maybe something is already in place that is currently affecting you and it will take a new law or policy to fix the problem. Perhaps the problem was brought to your attention by an organization you belong to, or maybe you just decided to take up the cause on your own. In any case, you know that you will have to engage in the public policy process in order to fix the problem.

The first thing you need to do is assess approximately how many people are affected by this issue and who they are. Even if you feel like you're the only aggrieved party, chances are that you are not. The more people you can identify as being sympathetic to the cause, the better. Is there an existing association or organization in place that you can join or enlist to your effort? If not, can you recruit enough interested people to start your own group? Believe it or not, it is not difficult or costly to form a legal organization dedicated to an issue, set of issues, or an industry. Most of the time this can be done on your Secretary of State's website in less than a day and for less than $100. Don't worry about obtaining a special IRS designation like 501(c)(3), because non-profit organizations are limited as to how much lobbying they can do. See Chapter 2 for more information about non-profits.

What are the benefits of having a group? Well, first of all the old theory about strength in numbers is paramount in politics. Numbers equal potential votes, and politicians love votes. Second, being part of a group can give you the appearance of being more credible and organized. The subsequent chapters of this book will take you through the steps in the process without regard to whether you are a band or a solo act, but my suggestion is that if you can recruit some brothers and sisters in arms, it can give you an advantage. Also, it's very possible that your efforts can cost a few bucks, and raising funds is much easier with more people to pass the hat to. Finally, if you are new to the political game, it will create familiarity with the officials you plan to meet with if you are part of or partnered up with an organization they have heard of before.

Another effective technique to jumpstart your campaign is to scan your local media to see of any stories have been written or broadcasted about your issue. Contact the journalist by phone or email and thank them for shedding light on the matter, and be sure to compliment them on their writing and thoroughness on the story. Then give a short but detailed background on why the issue is important to you, where you stand and why, and what action you plan to take in the near term. Then ask them if they would mind forwarding a letter to the editor you have drafted to the appropriate person at their outlet. Almost any media website will tell you how to submit a letter to the editor, but asking the reporter to help you implies trust and respect. Also, having the letter submitted from the inside gives you a better chance of the letter being read and published. If the reporter replies with just the contact info of where to send it instead of agreeing to send it for you, thank them for the help and then do the following: Send the letter to the contact given to you, copy the reporter on the email, and address the contact by saying that the reporter was kind enough to provide you with the editor's contact info. Be sure to mention that you got the idea to write the letter because you enjoyed the reporter's article and it inspired you to take a public stance on the issue. Many times, this will give you just as much of an advantage as the reporter forwarding the letter for you, and it can also create a relationship for future communications. Now all you need is a letter to the editor.

If you've never written one of these letters before, there's no need to be intimidated. You will no doubt know your issue, the pros and cons, and where you stand on it. If you are wondering about format, the best thing to do is look at other published letters from the same media outlet. Try to limit it to 500-650 words if possible. If your letter gets published, you automatically become a thought leader on the subject and have an arrow in your quiver going forward. Now you're off and running!

"All politics is local."

-*Former US House Speaker Tip O'Neil*

CHAPTER FOUR

IS MY ISSUE LOCAL, STATE, OR FEDERAL?

Regardless of whether you're dealing with a city, county, state, or federal issue, you first need to understand that all politics is local. This phrase, immortalized by former Speaker of the US House of Representatives Tip O'Neil, may very well be the truest statement ever made about American politics. Every elected official at every level of government represents a geographical area. Whether it is the City Council member who represents certain wards in the city or county, to the state legislator who often represents multiple counties, to the congressman who represents a large swath of the state, to the Senator or Governor who represents the entire state, you can bet that every one of these elected officials prioritize all issues based on how it affects their constituents.

You can't expect a congressman from rural Iowa to care about coastal restoration in Louisiana any more than you can expect a congressman from South Louisiana to care about ethanol subsidies. This works up and down the line. You can't get a city council member to get on board with appropriating funds for a public park in your neighborhood if he or she represents a district on the other side of town. One of the top things that an elected official cares about is the wants and needs of the people they represent, in other words, the registered voters in their district. The second thing they care about is the demands of their biggest donors. It may, at times, seem like there is a larger premium put on the wants of the donors, but in most cases the needs of the district come first. Politicians who pay more attention to the donors can soon find themselves out of a job, so the smart ones find a way to balance the two.

Raising funds for politicians is no doubt an important part of the public policy process. Whether right or wrong, it's just easier for them to remember who you are and what your issue is when you are a donor. You don't even necessarily have to be a large donor. Depending on the level of government, a contribution of anywhere from $100-500 can get the policy maker's attention. This can add up if your issue requires you to engage multiple elected officials, but every little bit helps. When booking an appointment, you can assume that the staff will cross-reference your name with the donor lists, and it always gives you an advantage if your name is on it.

One of the reasons people become cynical about politics is because they feel like only the wealthy who can afford to make campaign donations benefit from government. This is not necessarily true, because convincing a policy maker that an issue is important to a large percentage of his or her district can get you just as much action as writing a big check. This requires planning and organization, but if you follow the advice in this book, you will be surprised at what you can get your elected officials to do for you.

The first step in your planning process will be to determine the venue of jurisdiction for your issue. This simply refers to the level of government or regulatory authority that can affect the desired goal for your particular issue. It's not enough to contact your city council member if your goal is to secure federal funds for your state university, just like it's probably overkill to contact your US Senator about renaming the main street in your town (unless your town's main street happens to be a federal highway.) So, knowing which sandbox to play in is a necessary first step to ensure success for your campaign.

Local issues usually have their origin in and are governed by cities, townships, and counties. At this level, there is generally a mayor in the executive branch and a council in the legislative branch. In most cities and counties, the members of the legislative branch can be referred to as council members, aldermen, commissioners, or police jurors. The executives are usually referred to as mayors, presidents, judges (not the same as court room judges), or simply county executives. Laws passed at the municipal level are usually referred to as ordinances.

Underneath the structure of a municipal government, there are generally boards and committees of appointed individuals who make recommendations to the elected officials before they are voted upon. A common example of this is "planning and zoning." This committee decides everything from whether you can make an addition to your house to whether a developer can build a high-rise office tower. If you have an issue that requires zoning approval, it's always good to give your council member some heads up that you plan to present an item to any public committee before you get on the agenda. This way, if you run into any problems in the process, your councilmember will already be familiar with the background and can typically act more quickly on your behalf.

Some common issues that fall under the jurisdiction of a municipal government are:

- Zoning
- Local public safety
- Road and infrastructure maintenance (excludes state and federal highways)
- Rent laws
- Occupational licenses
- Sewerage and drainage issues

At the state level, the executive is the governor and the legislative branch is referred to as a legislature or an assembly. Most legislatures are bicameral, meaning they have two chambers. Nebraska has the only unicameral legislature in the United States, meaning they only have one legislative chamber. In the other 49 bicameral legislatures, the lower chamber is the House of Representatives, which will have the most members. The higher chamber is the Senate, which typically has fewer members.

The reason for the size differential between both chambers is that House districts are smaller than Senate districts. Laws passed at the state level are referred to as bills. Both chambers have many committees who meet while the legislature is in session, and some who meet regularly all year long. The committee structure is separated by industry and function, which makes it easy to find out which one will have jurisdiction over your issue. All bills and resolutions are considered at the committee level before being voted on by the full House and Senate, except in the rare occasion that the rules are suspended to allow an immediate floor vote.

At the executive level, the governor has a cabinet to oversee the various state departments and thousands of state employees. In addition, the governor will have his or her own staff who are vital to running the operations of the office, as well as directing traffic for those who wish to gain access to the governor and cabinet members. Much like the legislature, the state departments are separated by specific function, so it is easier to figure out which one might have jurisdiction over your issue.

Some common issues that fall under the jurisdiction of a state government are:

- Civil and criminal law
- Transportation and infrastructure
- Labor
- Healthcare
- Education
- Land and mineral rights
- Insurance
- Environment
- Agriculture
- State constitution
- Budgetary and fiscal matters

If you think that the state government is big, then you will quickly understand why the federal government is referred to as the 800-pound gorilla. The size and scope of the federal government is massive, and its powers are far reaching. It controls everything from who gets bombed to what the labels on the products in your refrigerator must say. Because Americans in every state pay federal taxes, cities and states all fight to get as much of those federal funds sent back home as possible. Because the money flows up then trickles back down, the federal government is in a position to use the carrot and stick approach to funding local governments.

Much of the process is bogged down in politics, and even more of it is controlled by unelected bureaucrats.

As far as the constitutional structure of the federal government, the executive branch is the President of the United States, the Vice President (who serves as the President of the Senate), and the various cabinet secretaries appointed by the president and confirmed by the Senate. As arguably the most visible and powerful person in the world, the president enjoys what is called the "bully pulpit", meaning that he can use the full weight of the White House to influence the rest of the government. Although there are three branches of government, complete with checks and balances, there is seldom a more influential member the federal government than the president.

The legislative branch is the U.S. Congress, which is a bicameral body made up of a House and Senate. There are 435 House members, which are divided up by each state's population, and 100 Senators, 2 from each state. The leader of the House is called the "Speaker". The Speaker gets to appoint all committee chairs as well as control the House calendar. The other leaders of the House are the Majority Leader (from the party holding the majority of members), the Majority Whip, the Minority Leader, and the Minority Whip. On the Senate side, the titular leader of the Senate is the

Vice President of the United States, but he usually only presides over the Senate on special occasions, and only casts a vote in the event of a 50-50 tie. The actual leader of the Senate is the Majority Leader, who has a Majority whip, and like the House there is a Minority Leader and Whip as well.

In addition to the leadership, there are many caucuses who wield varying degrees of influence in each chamber. Caucuses are groups of members who coalesce together for a common cause and can cast votes in a block. Caucuses can be formed based on state, region, industry, race, religion, ideology, or any other central cause that may bring a group of people together. Gaining the support of an influential caucus can greatly improve your chances of getting support and co-sponsors for your bill.

Some common issues that fall under the jurisdiction of the federal government are:

- Federal healthcare/ Medicare
- Education
- Immigration
- Military
- Budgetary
- Terrorism
- Bill of Rights
- Transportation and infrastructure
- Interior

- Social Security
- Labor and wages
- Taxes
- Judicial appointments

One common denominator across all levels of government is the third branch, the judiciary. The judicial branch of government has oversight of all laws existing, as well as new laws passed, to ensure that they do not violate the constitution. Any law can be challenged in court on its constitutional merit, and a judge can decide whether a violation exists. Appeals to the judicial decisions can be made through the state district and supreme courts, federal courts, and all the way to the U.S. Supreme Court. Once the Supreme Court decides a case, the decision becomes the law of the land and cannot be altered by the executive or legislative branch. The only way the decision can then be overturned is if the Supreme Court reverses itself.

"When you can do the common things of life in an uncommon way, you will command the attention of the world."

-George Washington Carver

Laws and Sausage
You never want to see either one get made!

CHAPTER FIVE

HOW CAN I CREATE AWARENESS FOR MY ISSUE?

If a tree falls down in the middle of the forest, does it make any noise? This is an old riddle which makes the point that if nobody notices something, did it really happen? Of course, we assume that the falling tree makes noise because it does every time someone is around to watch it fall. But if nobody witnessed the event, we can't say with absolute certainty that it made a noise. The advertising industry was built on this very concept. The same goes for political messaging, if nobody hears about your cause, then it may as well not exist.

If your issue is controversial or has recently gained media attention, whether traditional or social, it is imperative to ride the publicity wave and attempt to turn the narrative in your favor. Whenever you see a news story about your issue, whether in print, on TV, or on radio, the news organization in question almost always has a digital version of the story on their website. It's important for you, and anybody you can get to do so, to post in the "comments" section under the story. This is a free technique that gives you the opportunity to share your opinion with the readers immediately after they read the story. If enough comments are made to support your position, it's possible to sway that reader's opinion in your direction. When posting comments, however, it's important not to rant or be offensive to the perceived opposition of your issue. Use as many facts as possible, and when possible, include website links that people can click on and find information that backs up your claims. You must come across as sober and credible or you will turn people off, and potentially damage your efforts.

If there hasn't been a lot of attention on your issue, you can create some by writing a letter to the editor in your local paper (See Chapter 3), starting a Facebook campaign, creating a Twitter hashtag, or starting a blog.

Facebook is a great way to get a message out quickly and at a relatively low cost. The more friends you have on Facebook, then obviously, the more people will potentially see your post. When you are posting a message that you would like for as many people as possible to see, you go to the upper left corner of your post and look for the drop down menu that lets you decide whether only your friends or the general public can see it. You want to select "Public", that way the potential reach of your message goes far beyond just your confirmed Facebook friends.

After posting a message on Facebook, you might notice an option under the dialogue box called "Boost Post." This is a way that you can increase the reach of your post for a fee. The great thing about the Facebook model is that you can choose a lot of different filters to decide what kind of people you want to target. You can choose by gender, age range, geography, hobbies and interests (which is important to finding those who might be sympathetic to your cause), and other subcategories. You can start off with a wide range of people and drill down until you have your most desirable audience targeted. My favorite part is that you get to set your own budget, and as you set the dollar amount you're willing to spend and the parameters of people you want to target, it will give you an estimate of what your potential reach will be. I have created Facebook boosted posts where I was able to reach up to 200,000 people for only a couple hundred dollars. I believe that in a grassroots effort, Facebook is the best bang for your buck.

In addition to paid ads, you can search Facebook for people, groups, and organizations who are posting similar topics to yours, and you can usually post to their pages and potentially find more like-minded people for your cause. If these people have many friends and followers of their own, you can piggy-back on their network to promote your message and identify yourself as a partner and sympathizer to the issue. Finally, whenever you make a post on Facebook about your cause, whether it's on your page, in a boosted post, or on someone else's page, ALWAYS make the request within the post for people to share it. People can click the "Share" button underneath your post, and it automatically reposts the message on their own page. This is another very effective technique to spread your message across Facebook for free. Usually, your own Facebook friends are the most likely to share your posts because they know you and want to help you out. But to encourage people whom you may not know or are not in your network to share your post, my recommendation is to begin your message with "PLEASE SHARE!!!", then go ahead and type out your message. The all-caps and the request to share up front gets people's attention, makes them more likely to read the post, and also more likely to share the post.

Twitter is another highly effective way to get your message out to a mass audience very quickly, but it does have limitations. First, you are limited to only 140 characters per post. Second, the only free way to get people beyond those who follow your Twitter feed to see your message is to get others to retweet, similar to sharing a Facebook post. Twitter does have opportunities to purchase ads, or "sponsored tweets", but I don't find them as targeted or economical. Your best bet for a tweet to go viral is to get a celebrity who has a lot of Twitter followers to retweet your message for you. Since this is not likely, you should try the strategy of creating a hashtag campaign. This is when you put a pound sign before a word or catch phrase that, if enough people use, can get your tweets "trending." An example would be **#LawsAndSausage**. Trending refers to a word, name, or phrase that is being talked about a lot on Twitter, usually at such a high rate that it gets ranked as a popular subject. If you create a hashtag for your cause and can get as many people as possible to use the hashtag in all of their tweets, then you have a chance at getting your topic to trend and be seen by more Twitter users.

The final recommendation to gain some attention to your cause is to start a blog. My suggestion would be to search the internet for an existing blog or message board that shares your views on your issue. There is a very good chance that one already exists, and you will save time by posting to an active message board or offering to submit an article for consideration to be published on a blog. Most bloggers are always looking for free content, and a popular source for that content is to have guest columnists. In addition, if the blog is sympathetic to your cause, they probably already have a built-in audience that you can get in front of by having your article published.

If you cannot find any sources online to join forces with, then you should consider starting your own blog. The most popular platform for blogging is WordPress. WordPress is an online tool that has a step-by-step system to create a website or a blog. There are other similar platforms that you can use, and I am not promoting one over another, but WordPress just happens to currently be the most popular. Internet search results are generated by algorithms that scour the internet for the words and phrases you are searching for. By having a blog on a popular platform, when people search for words and phrases that are germane to your issue, there is a good chance that your blog will show up in the results, and ultimately bring the searcher to your site. It's also a good way to build a community of like-minded people that you can summon for action to make calls, send e-mails, and post to social media in support of your cause. The more content your blog has, the better chance it has of showing up in search engine results. So, when you are just starting out and don't have much content, you can post links to your blog in the comments section of news articles and message boards connected to your issue. Some admins consider this technique spamming and might disallow your link, but most will probably allow it if the information you link is relevant and agreeable. Nevertheless, this can get some initial traffic to your blog, and possibly help you recruit some guest columnists that can help you add to your content library.

"The essential ingredient of politics is timing."

-*Pierre Trudeau*

CHAPTER SIX

HOW IMPORTANT IS THE TIMING OF MY CAMPAIGN?

We've all heard the expressions "Timing is everything" and "Strike while the iron is hot." These two notions are as critical in politics as any other. In the last chapter, we discussed some techniques on how you can capitalize on media attention and how to create some of your own. The hope is that your efforts have now either caused a follow up to existing press about your issue, or your grassroots efforts have caused enough of a stir to bring your issue to a boil. But what do you do if you catch a break and not only the media, but elected officials start to take notice of your issue? What if they are on the other side of you? How can you make sure you stand out as a thought leader on the subject? How can you pitch yourself as a resource for information that can be called on to testify at a public hearing?

A few years ago, my firm signed with Uber Technologies to be their lobbyist for the State of Louisiana. They really wanted to be in New Orleans because of the huge tourism industry there, but were skeptical of the political climate in the city. New Orleans politics has a reputation of being more "Northern Caribbean" than "Southern United States." The first thing I explained to them was that New Orleans was an old soul who didn't take to change easily, and that it would probably take some time. In any case, I was confident that we could get it done. I set up a few initial meetings at city hall to take the temperature of the council and the mayor. The initial response was mostly positive, but they had the same concerns I did...the taxi industry. The city had just passed a lot of tough and expensive regulations on the taxis about two years earlier, and it was a public and brutal fight that the city won. Given these circumstances, I knew that the taxi industry would not be happy about the introduction of ride-sharing right after taking this very recent punch in the gut. So, in other words, the timing couldn't have been worse. If I wanted to fully bring the city officials to the water, I was going to have to find them some political cover.

So, after identifying our strengths and weaknesses, I started to look at the strengths and weaknesses of the opposition. Their number one weakness was, of course, the public. I knew that most people I talked to were not fans of cab drivers, but it wasn't until I got into this battle that I realized just how much the people of New Orleans despised the taxi industry as a whole. Even with the new regulations, the cars were dirty, the drivers were dirtier, and if you called the cab dispatch to come pick you up at home, you'd be lucky if they showed up within an hour or even on the same day. Simply put, New Orleans was ripe for ride sharing, but a straight public relations campaign wasn't going to be enough to get me across the goal line.

Then it happened, I caught a huge break. To prepare for their eventual entrance into the market (they had confidence in me), Uber started placing ads to recruit drivers throughout the city. The city's transportation director, who turned out to be a rabid anti-Uber activist, decided to make an official response when he saw the ads. He took it upon himself to draft a letter, on his official city letterhead, to Uber demanding that they cease and desist all activities in New Orleans. Here was the problem: Uber wasn't operating in New Orleans yet. He basically sent a letter to a private business and threatened them with arrest if they came to the New Orleans, not exactly a welcome wagon.

I had a sneaking suspicion that this guy had not sought nor received permission from his superiors to send a letter like this, especially given the fact that the language mirrored the diplomatic skills of the Mongol Horde. So, I got a copy of the letter from Uber, sent it to the news director of my favorite local TV station, and we were off and running. They ran the letter as the lead on the evening news, and within a day or two the rest of the local media was talking about Uber. The mayor wasn't thrilled that I had gone to the media without calling him first, but I had to do what was best for my client. Across the hall however, city council members weren't mad at me, they were mad about the letter. Suddenly, I had most of the council, most of the local media, as well as most of the public on my side.

It wasn't a done deal yet, but I had just injected my political capital with steroids. Like I said, nothing happens fast in New Orleans, and that especially goes for passing ordinances. Even when the council finally agreed on draft language, the general procedure calls for at least two different public hearings with a 21-day holdover before they could legally even take a vote. I had to do something to motivate them.

75 miles to the west of New Orleans lies the capital city of Baton Rouge. Baton Rouge had become a densely-populated city after Hurricane Katrina when tens of thousands of people fled for higher ground. Traffic is a huge problem in the city, and cab service is nearly non-existent. Additionally, there were a pair of young, forward thinking members of the Baton Rouge Metro Council who I was confident would like the idea of bringing Uber into their city. The cherry on top was the fact that council procedures were such that ordinances could be passed relatively quickly, sometimes in a manner of weeks. I met with these two young Turks at Baton Rouge city hall, and they were on board within minutes. I quickly got them a draft copy of model legislation for ride-sharing, and it was introduced at the following council meeting. I

made the rounds with the rest of the council to make sure that I could whip up at least 5 more votes (7 were needed to pass the full council), as well as make sure the mayor wasn't going to oppose the measure. It didn't take long before I had 7 commitments, and the mayor's office said that they would not take a position on the ordinance. This just meant that they wouldn't interfere either way, which in some cases is as good as an endorsement. The ordinance was on the agenda for the very next council meeting, and after about an hour of debate, it passed with 8 votes, which is 1 more than I needed. So, just like that, Baton Rouge had beaten New Orleans in the ride-sharing race.

That didn't sit well with a lot of New Orleans politicians, since they see the city as the most progressive in the state. Within a few weeks, the New Orleans council had agreed on an ordinance draft that was introduced and referred to committee. As predicted, it took multiple public hearings for us to get to a point where they could vote on the ordinance. New Orleans only has 7 council members, so I only needed 4 votes. The original ordinance passed 4-3. Over the next year, there were several cleanup measurers that needed to be passed in order to posture the law in a way that made the city attorneys happy, but we ultimately got it done.

As you can see, passing laws is a process with many twists and turns. But I hope this example shows you how to take advantage of timing, take advantage of a lucky break, and how to sometimes make your own luck.

"When you must break the law, do it to seize power: in all other cases observe it."

-Julius Caesar

CHAPTER SEVEN

WHEN AND HOW DO I SCHEDULE MY FIRST MEETING?

While the preceding chapters of this book have focused on setting the stage for your meetings with public officials, the reality is that you can request a meeting any time you want. However, I spent an entire chapter talking about timing so that you can understand the benefits of proper planning. There may be some emergency or deadline regarding your issue that requires you to meet with a policy maker right away, and that's ok. But if you have the time to employ the tactics covered so far, then my recommendation is to hold off on face to face meetings until you've had a chance to soften the ground. But if you've done your homework and feel you are ready to start meeting with your elected representatives, then let's go!

By now you should know where to start, that is, whether your issue is local, state, or federal. It is also relevant whether there is already pending legislation regarding your issue, or whether you plan to propose new legislation. Your strategy will differ based on these factors, so you should be making a list that will help you know which path to take in the next few chapters.

Obviously, the lower the level of government you plan to target, the easier it should be to get in front of the policy maker who can help you. If you live in a small town and need to meet with a city council member, they may not even have an office or any staff. In cases like this, it's possible that you can call these officials at home or just go knock on their door. For larger cities, the members of the council and the mayor will have a staff of gatekeepers you will have to go through to set the meeting.

The first thing you will want to do is find the office you want to meet with online. These days, there are very few organized governments who don't have a website. Hopefully, your city or county will have a website that lists contact info for the official as well as names of staffers and their function. This way you will know who to ask for when you call, and it creates a more relaxed feeling for the person you contact. If the website isn't detailed, you can call and ask to speak to the scheduler. When the scheduler gets on the phone, you professionally introduce yourself, your organization if you have one, and the reason for the meeting request. You don't have to get in to a long diatribe about all your feelings on the issue, because the scheduler won't care. But they are the gatekeeper, so be polite, professional, and make them feel important. They may or may not ask a lot of questions, if they do then be succinct but informative so you sound like a pro. They may suggest meeting with another staff member initially, don't be offended by this. It's not uncommon to go through a few folks before getting to the boss. Again, this usually only happens in larger local governments, but you should be prepared for it.

If the scheduler does suggest an initial staffer meeting, tell them that will be fine, after all, you're inside the city gates. But also, mention that if a "pop-in" is possible, then you would appreciate it. A pop-in is when the boss comes into the room during the meeting, says hello to everyone, maybe stays for a few minutes and gets an elevator pitch from you, and then thanks you for coming. But don't worry if the pop-in doesn't happen. If the meeting goes well, then you can count on a follow up meeting where you will almost assuredly get more face time with the policy maker.

If your target is a state legislator, then the process is similar but with a few variables. Remember, the more people that an elected official represents, the busier they are, and the more people they have to meet with every day. If the legislature is not in session, then you will set up the appointment much like you did at the city or county level. Most state legislators are part-time, only in a few states is it a full-time job. This means that while not in session, these officials will likely be working in their full-time positions, so you should keep this in mind when you are trying to get on their schedule. If the legislature is in session, it is generally easier to catch the member in between committee meetings, having a page call them off the floor, or you might even see them in the hallway or cafeteria. The difference is that you will have far less of their time and attention, so your elevator pitch should be rehearsed and refined. The good news is that in these micro-meetings, you generally get to talk to the member without their handlers around. If you are dealing with a particular bill, make sure you know what the bill number is. It's a good idea to write the bill number on the back of your business card so that when the member gives it to their staffer later, they will know what you talked about. If you are trying to propose legislation, it is better to do so before the session starts. If the timing wasn't possible, you will need to meet with staff to get a bill drafted, that's assuming the official has agreed to author it. You will also want to be mindful of any filing deadlines.

At the federal level, the process is similar to that of a state legislature, but again with a few variables. First, although Congress recesses a lot, they meet year around. Second, you have to decide whether you will be asking to meet the congressman or senator in D.C. or in the district. If you can't make the trip to Capitol Hill, then you need to be prepared to wait until the official is back home. If you're going to D.C., call the scheduler as soon as you know what your travel plans are so they have enough lead time to get you on the calendar. It is not uncommon to be offered an appointment 2 to 3 weeks out from the date of request.

In congress, security is much tighter than in most city and state buildings, so you may have less chance of a random meeting. It is possible to run into a member walking through the halls of the congressional office buildings, but usually they are heading to a meeting or to a vote. Either way, you should be prepared to get no more than 30 seconds of face time during these encounters.

Whichever level you are working at, remember that the staffers make the world go around. They control who gets access and who doesn't. They are generally younger people who don't get paid a lot of money, so if you are rude they will not be very motivated to help you. It's always been my policy to treat staff like royalty, and if the person I'm in contact with leading up to the meeting is not visible when I walk in the office, I'll always ask to see them just so I can thank them in person for their help. This goes a long way, and that staffer will remember you every time you call or e-mail in the future.

"It usually takes me two or three days to come up with an impromptu speech."

-*Mark Twain*

CHAPTER EIGHT

MY MEETING IS SCHEDULED, NOW WHAT?

Time to prepare. The proper preparation for your meeting is just as, if not more important than carrying out the meeting itself. The first thing you should do is find out how to speak the lawmaker's language. What do I mean by that? Well, every policy maker has his or her own hobbies, likes, and interests. Do some research online, or ask people who might have a relationship with the lawmaker to find out what they like to do when they aren't working. Do they have a favorite sports team? Do their kids excel in dance or music? Chances are, if they attended a college that has a perennially good football or basketball team, he or she is probably a big fan. It's usually not hard to find some type of inside information, but if all else fails, you can look around the office when you get there. Somewhere in the lobby there are usually pictures and other types of memorabilia that can clue you in on things that are important to the lawmaker. If not, then the personal office will definitely have items like this. Find something you can identify with yourself, and use that as an ice breaker to start the conversation when you first meet. This will create a more relaxed atmosphere by establishing familiarity, because after all, you are still a stranger.

You also want to have prepared what I have previously referred to as your "elevator pitch." This is a condensed version of your issue, who it affects, and what you propose that the lawmaker does about it. It's called the elevator pitch because theoretically, you should be able to deliver the entire presentation within the span of a trip down an elevator. Now, this is hyperbolic, and you will generally get a little more time than that for a scheduled meeting. But you should understand that these policy makers meet with dozens of people every day, and they appreciate brevity. After introductions and your planned ice breaker, you should be prepared to go right into your "ask." Try to have a personal story, facts and figures, and examples of how the issue affects his or her district. If you yourself do not live in the lawmaker's district, plan to bring someone who does. If that is not possible, try to get someone in the district to pen a letter for you endorsing your position, and plan to hand deliver the letter. Make sure that person signs it and puts their home address under their name, so that it can be verified that they live in the district.

Finally, have a "leave behind" that you will give a copy of to the lawmaker and any staffers in the room. To be safe, bring at least 10 copies. They will never go to waste because this probably won't be your last meeting. The "leave behind" should be one page. It should be very succinct and use layman's terms. Many first timers like to leave a binder or a folder with multiple documents in them. Trust me when I tell you that there is very little chance that the whole thing will ever be read. A one pager that is bullet pointed has a much better chance of being read, and they might read it right in front of you during the meeting. Remember, these policy makers deal with lot of people about lots of different issues. They don't want the labor pains, they just want the baby.

You'll want to find out where the lawmaker stands on your issue. There are three basic positions they can take on any given issue: they can support it, oppose it, or be undecided. Once again, search online to see if they have taken a public stance on the issue. If you can't find anything, you can call their office in advance (you should do this prior to making the appointment) and ask a staffer what the position of their boss is. Most of the time they will know and be happy to tell you, but if not, they will take your information and have someone call you back. Once you know what you're up against, you can customize your elevator pitch according to what type of reaction you anticipate the lawmaker will have when you meet with them.

If they support your issue, you should immediately plan to ask if they would consider sponsoring legislation. If an ordinance or bill has already been drafted or filed, ask the lawmaker if he or she will consider being a co-author. Tell them that you feel having their name on the legislation would greatly increase the chance of passage. Go through your elevator pitch the same as you would for anyone, but add in a series of phrases like "As you know..." and "I'm sure you would agree that..." and "With your leadership, and the leadership of your like-minded colleagues...". This will let the lawmaker know that when it comes time to do battle, he or she will have a team to back them up.

If they are against your issue, you will need solid information as to why they should reconsider. Cite some high-profile experts, or even better, one of their colleagues who share your views on the issue. It's important not to come off as adversarial just because the lawmaker doesn't agree with you. Be respectful and use phrases like, "I respect where you're coming from, but perhaps you haven't had a chance to see this statistic yet...", or "I see why would feel that way, and I used to feel the same until...". Let them know that you are an advocate, not a zealot. Winston Churchill said, "A fanatic is someone who can't change their mind and won't change the subject." Be polite, be informative, show respect, but also show conviction.

If you are meeting with an undecided lawmaker, your first task will be to ascertain why he or she is undecided. Many times, it could be as simple as they have not had time to study the issue enough to take a position yet. This is when you become as asset, because you are an expert and are there to deliver a host of information. If they are undecided because the issue is controversial, or if it is drawing a lot of differing opinions from their constituents, this is when it is the most helpful to have that constituent with you (if you are not one), or have that letter from a constituent that you will hand deliver. It could also be that your competition, that is, an advocate who represents the other side of your issue has already met with the lawmaker, and he or she is waiting to hear your side before making a decision. A big part of your preparation should involve studying the platform of your opposition and developing counterarguments to their ask. Whether you are first or last in the order of meetings, you want to be remembered as the most prepared and informed.

Now that you have your initial preparation done, you'll want to, as accurately as possible, anticipate the dynamics and flow of the meeting. The best way to do this is by rehearsing, or role playing. I've been a professional political operative for over twenty years, and I still rehearse meeting before they take place, particularly when I will be meeting with a policy maker for the first time. Even if you have notes, you can still forget things because sometimes you are forced to deliver a lot of information in a short period of time. If you plan to have one or more people joining you at the meeting, you'll want to decide who will cover which part of your elevator pitch. Nothing is more annoying to a policy maker than listening to people fumble and talk over each other. Have someone play the policy maker, and pretend that they are either opposed or undecided as to your issue. Have them go through all the potential objections you can think of, and work to overcome those objections just like in a sales call. After all, there is a lot of salesmanship involved in lobbying! Also, when you practice overcoming potential objections, you can avoid being tripped up or looking like a deer in the headlights. Practice your lines out loud, that way when you repeat them at the actual meeting, they will sound natural and familiar to you. By answering every objection quickly and thoroughly, you will come off as an expert and have a better chance of swaying the lawmaker to your side.

"The best argument against democracy is spending five minutes with the average voter."

-*Winston Churchill*

CHAPTER NINE

IT'S MEETING DAY, AM I READY?

If you have followed the steps outlined so far in this book, then you are ready for your meeting!

Chances are, during the course of preparing for and setting up this meeting, you have probably had one primary contact either by phone or by e-mail coordinating the meeting for you. It's very possible that the meeting has been rescheduled a few times. Don't get annoyed if that happens by the way, it can actually generate a couple of benefits for you. First, it creates more interaction between you and the scheduler, which just means that the scheduler is more likely to remember you in the future. Second, when a meeting has to be rescheduled or postponed, the person who informs you has the unenviable duty of delivering the bad news, and they are sometimes the recipient of flak from the appointee. By being polite to a fault, you are reassuring the staffer that you are an empathetic and professional person who understands that it isn't their fault when trains don't run on time. These little nuances are a valuable part of the relationship-building process.

When I finally walk into a lawmaker's office, the first thing I do is introduce myself and tell the person greeting me what time my appointment is scheduled for. Then I ask if the person who has been my primary contact is available. If they are, I tell them that I just wanted to thank them in person for being such a big help. Anytime you get to single out a staffer for a job well done, take the opportunity. This will solidify the relationship and show that you genuinely appreciate their efforts. Sometimes the person is not available, in which case I leave my card and ask if the greeter will do me a personal favor and give the scheduler my card and thank them for me. They will appreciate the gesture. In some cases, the person who scheduled you will be in the meeting, and they are still wrapping up the appointment prior to yours. This is the best-case scenario, because you will be able to show your gratitude in front of everyone in the meeting, and usually in front of their boss. Who doesn't like being praised by a customer in front of their boss? Score!

Whether you meet people in scattered fashion or all at once, the proper etiquette is to introduce yourself (and your organization name if applicable), then let the rest of your group introduce themselves. It's not as personal when someone else rattles off the names of everyone in the group, plus it lets your team feel more involved in the meeting from the start. Here's another trick that I always use: It's customary, when you meet someone for the first time, to say something like, "Nice to meet you." It's courteous, but common. Remember, you want to stand out from the crowd, right? I always, regardless of who it is, say, "It's nice to see you (name or title)." Why? Because I meet with so many lawmakers and staffers every day that it's possible I have met someone before without remembering it. Political staffers tend to rotate between offices, especially at the state and federal level, so I might remember them but just don't associate them with that office. In any case, I hate it when people I have met before don't remember me. It makes me feel like I didn't do enough to stand out at our last meeting, and it reflects poorly on me. I know that they don't mean any disrespect, but I can't help but take it personally. When you say, "Good to see you," it's an appropriate greeting whether you are meeting someone for the first time, and it also covers you if you have previously met but don't remember. Here's the other catch, when a person hears "Nice to see you," they almost always question themselves as to whether or not they have met you before. They think, "Oh my goodness, have I met this guy but I just don't remember? I just said nice to *meet* you, and he said nice to *see* you. I feel so bad." Trust me, that person will go out of their way to remember you again so they don't feel awkward in the future. Try this technique, it works.

So, you're finally in the room with the lawmaker. You've got your notes, you've got your elevator pitch ready, you have stack of leave behinds, and you have your game face on. Don't get so excited that you launch right into your ask. Remember, ice breaker first! Whatever ice breaker you have chosen, make sure it isn't patronizing. Don't talk to someone from Iowa about corn, don't talk to someone from Idaho about potatoes. Don't talk about the weather. It's corny, and everyone in the room has been outside today, they know what the weather is like. Make it personal and relatable, and make sure it is a subject you can talk intelligently about. Then, smoothly segue into your ask. Stick to the plan that you rehearsed. It's very easy to get excited in the moment and forget your preparation. If it helps, draft a sequential outline as to how you would like your presentation to flow, complete with who will say what. This will help get you on track in the event that you draw a blank. Prepare for the lawmaker or staffer to ask questions along the way. This is a good thing, because it means that they are listening and looking for clarity on the subject. When you get through the pitch and there appear to be no more questions, just say, "We want to thank you so much for your time, and I'd like to stay in touch with your staff in order to keep them up to date on any developments (or something along those lines)". Start saying your goodbyes, and maybe make one more quick reference to the ice breaker (assuming it went well). This can help bolster that memorable quality you hope to leave behind. Make sure you collect business cards from everyone in the meeting, as a citizen activist you should start a rolodex just for policy makers and staff. On your way out the door, thank everyone you come in contact with. You're a pro, and want to be remembered as one.

Now, here's a very important thing to remember immediately after you leave the office: Don't talk about the meeting you just had with your group. Don't talk about it in the hallway, don't talk about it in the elevator, don't talk about it in the lobby, don't even talk about it in the parking lot. If your group feels the need to download after the meeting, go off site to a restaurant, coffee shop, or back to your office. The reason? You ever know who is listening or where they might be listening. A random person anywhere in the building could be a staffer, a friend of a staffer, or a friend of the lawmaker, and the wrong conversation overheard can absolutely unwind all the work you just did. I have seen this happen on more than one occasion, so always be mindful of your surroundings. Finally, don't pine over how the meeting went, if the meeting ended with all smiles and handshakes, then it went great!

Depending on the scope of your issue, you may have to hold meetings with multiple policy makers. If this is the case, duplicate the process described in this chapter until you have sufficiently made your case to all of the stakeholders that will be involved in the process. The harder of a sell your idea is, the harder you will have to work to gain commitments from members to vote for it.

"One of the consequences of refusing to participate in politics is that you end up being governed by your inferiors."

-Plato

CHAPTER TEN

WHAT DO I DO AFTER MY MEETINGS?

After meeting with every policy maker who you think can and will assist your campaign, then you are ready to see exactly how the sausage is made. The process will vary between local, state, and federal government. But a common denominator is that each will have separate branches, and all are compartmentalized. By that, I mean that there is usually an executive, a legislative, and a judicial branch at each level. It also means that underneath the government is a host of departments, committees, and subcommittees. In the judicial branch, there are usually small claims court, traffic court, city court, state court, and federal courts in local districts. For the purposes of this book, we'll go over common procedures that executive and legislative branches usually adhere to.

As stated in previous chapters, things may be much less formal and the process can move much faster in smaller markets, but this chapter will operate under the assumption that you are dealing with a medium to large sized municipality. Before attempting to create and pass legislation, you will probably have
to meet with a city department or committee. You may have to submit a formal petition to get on the agenda, but generally the process to get on the agenda is not an arduous one. If your issue doesn't require you to meet with one of these departments or committees, you are probably going straight to the council with your proposal. Still, most councils

have breakout committees that deal with specific ordinances. Some examples are transportation, public health, environmental, permitting, criminal justice, community development, etc. Once your ordinance is read into the calendar, it will be referred to one of these committees. The committees will generally meet on a different day than the full council meeting, and usually count as the first public hearing (some laws require a certain number of public hearings before a vote is taken). The author of the ordinance will give a synopsis of what the intent of the proposal is, and field questions from the members of the committee. The committee will also hear public testimony on the ordinance, which will be your opportunity to give your elevator pitch in public. If there is a full docket that day, or if there are a lot of people signed up to give public testimony, you may be limited to just a few minutes to speak. If you have a lot of information to give, bring other people with you and divide up the pitch between you, since you will each be given a few minutes to speak. Make sure you go in order so to the committee it sounds like one, unified speech.

After all the questions have been asked and the public testimony given, the chair of the committee will call for a vote. It is also possible that a motion can be made to defer the ordinance to another meeting, which is a delay tactic. This usually only happens when an issue is controversial and draws a heated debate. Another thing the committee can do is vote to refer the ordinance to the full council without recommendation. This means that the committee itself is avoiding action and relying on the full council to make a decision. If the committee decides to vote against the ordinance, that usually means that it will not be considered by the full council and is, at least for the moment, dead. If the ordinance makes it to the full council, then another opportunity for testimony and debate will be given, and this counts as another public hearing. If a third public hearing is required, then the council may not call for a vote, and choose to do so at a future meeting. Once a vote is called, then the council can vote yes, no, defer to a later date, or return to the calendar. Returning to the calendar is the same as death for an ordinance. It basically means that the council did not want to be on record voting for or against it, but reserves the right to call it back from the calendar. Only in the rarest of circumstances are they called back. It's the political equivalent of punting in football.

At the state legislative level, the ordinances are usually called bills or resolutions. The process is similar, as there are committee meetings which take place before going to a full vote of either the house or senate. But with a bicameral legislature, each chamber has their own committees. Most house committees have counterpart committees in the senate, and vice versa. This means twice the work. The author of the bill will introduce it to the committee, and the panel will ask questions of the author. After this is concluded, the committee will take public testimony. In most cases, you will have to fill out a card or sign in sheet with the sergeant at arms in order to be called to testify. Once again, you will give your testimony and answer any questions the committee might have. At the state level, committees generally won't refer a bill to the full body without reporting it favorably, meaning without a majority vote. They can also defer, return to the calendar, or vote the measure down. A deferment is not always a bad thing, because if they wanted to kill it they would have either voted it down or returned it to the calendar. But if they don't announce the date on which the bill will be reconsidered, it could remain deferred indefinitely.

If a bill or resolution originates in the house, it will go through the house committee process, and if reported favorably, will go on the calendar to be considered by the full house. The Speaker will control when and if the measure will appear on the "order of the day', which is akin to the daily docket. If your bill doesn't get on the order of the day within a week or so, you may want to check to see if there is a reason such as a controversy or objection from a powerful member or group to the bill. The Speaker may be holding up the bill until some negotiating can be done. It can also be that due to prioritizing, your bill was temporarily delayed. While this is not common, it is worth mentioning so that you be prepared for it. At this point in the process, you are now tracking your bill through the sausage maker and you want to be aware of any procedural roadblocks. The first thing you should do is talk to the sponsor, because they can inquire as to the status. The next step is talk to the chairman of the committee that reported the bill favorably, he or she will have influence with the speaker and can find out what any potential problem may be.

Once the floor vote is scheduled, it will be called from the order by the clerk and the sponsor will go to the podium and introduce the bill. The sponsor will then give a brief digest on the bill's intentions and field any questions from members. Once debate has concluded, a vote will be called. Some legislatures have rules which state that if a bill raises taxes or seeks to amend the state constitution, it must receive a two-thirds vote of each body. But in most cases, the bill needs a simple majority vote to pass. If it fails, then you live to fight another day. Typically, if a non-controversial bill is approved by a committee, it should face little resistance in a floor vote. Once passed, the Speaker and the house clerk will sign the bill and present it to the senate for consideration.

While the senate has its own rules and procedures, the progress of your bill will likely travel down a similar path that it took in the house. It will be introduced, then referred to committee, have a committee hearing, get voted on, and if passed it will go to the full senate for debate and a vote. Since the sponsor of the bill is a house member, he or she will ask a senator to handle the bill for them since house members will not be authorized to participate in senate activities. The senate can be a different animal than the house. I mentioned the different rules and procedures, but there is often a different culture as well. Senates tend to be more deliberative, and thus they don't always move as fast as the house. The only advantage is that there are fewer senators than house members, so there are less votes needed to pass your bill. If you get lucky, your bill will pass the committee and full senate without being amended. As stated many times before, the less controversial your bill is, the more "under the radar" it will fly and draw less attention. If your bill is passed by the full senate, then it will be on its way to the governor for signature. If your bill is amended in any way by the senate, even if it is to add a comma in a single sentence, then things get a little tricky.

Amendments are simply changes to a bill that can involve language, changes in numerical values, punctuation, or may change the entire intent of the bill. An amended bill also means that the version passed by the house has been altered, so even of the full senate passes the bill as amended, it is still not yet ready for executive signature. The versions of a bill passed by the house and senate must be exactly the same, down to the last detail, before the bill can be certified by the legislature. In the case of an amendendment, the bill will then be sent to what is called a "conference committee." In a conference committee, the Speaker of the House and President of the Senate will choose three or four members from each chamber to get together and negotiate the language in each version until each side has a matching version. The committees are generally made up of the bill's sponsor, the senator who handled the bill for the sponsor, the chairman from each committee, and perhaps a member of the leadership from each side. These conferences are usually held out of the public eye, and if an agreement is reached, will produce what is known as a conference report. Since you will not be able to attend the conference, it is important to find out who will serve in the conference so that you can lobby them on behalf of your bill. This is especially important if your bill contains amendments you don't agree with. The conference report will then be sent to the house and senate for approval. The conference report, however, bypasses the committee process this time and goes straight to a floor vote on each side. Conference reports are rarely rejected since they have been debated at length and it contains a version of the bill that both sides felt they could live with. When the report is passed by both the house and senate, the final bill (often referred to as the "engrossed" bill) is sent to the governor for signature. Once the governor signs the bill, it is now set to be become law. Most states have a specific date every year, many times the first day of their fiscal year, when all new laws go into effect. Some laws, depending on their nature, become effective immediately upon the governor's signature. When your bill is first drafted, it will usually denote whether it becomes law immediately upon signature or not.

The U.S. Congress has very similar procedures as state legislatures when comes to how a bill becomes a law, but it is far more difficult and takes a lot longer at this level. There are far more members in each chamber, for starters. Secondly, the members are from all different parts of the country instead of being from different parts of the same state. This creates a larger mixture of cultures, ideologies, and priorities. Third, there are many more committees, subcommittees, special committees, select committees, and joint committees than in a state legislature. Finally, there are infinitely more bills and resolutions introduced at the federal level every year than in any one state.

If your issue is one that needs to be handled at the federal level, you should probably consider bringing in some help. There are interest groups, trade organizations, and associations for nearly every type of industry and issue you can think of. Unless you are breaking some kind of innovative new ground in politics, chances are there is a group in Washington, D.C. that is already working on the cause. Use the internet and social media to find out which one of these groups is the best fit for you and contact them, these types of organizations will almost always welcome new members with open arms. They can also share research and resources that you may not have seen yet. Finally, they will likely have either in-house or contract lobbyists already working on the hill on behalf of the cause. If you still feel like you want to go it alone, here are some things to consider first: if you don't live in D.C., you will incur a lot of travel expenses because it will take multiple trips over long periods of time to get any legislation passed. You can certainly visit your congressional delegation while they are home in their district offices, but without being in D.C., it is very hard to help your bill move through the process. Congress has far more road blocks for legislation than city councils or state legislatures do. It's easier to push a Clydesdale up a flight of stairs than to get a bill through congress.

Now that you have been sufficiently warned, here's how you get started. Begin by using the techniques in chapters 8 and 9 to set and execute meetings with your local congressman and senators. Lawmakers at the federal level have larger staffs, so your interaction with the staff will be more important than ever. Congressional staff normally consists of a few young people and possibly some interns, but at the legislative director and chief of staff level, you will be dealing with savvy professionals. People don't get those jobs without knowing their way around capitol hill, so you shouldn't feel slighted when you are asked to meet with staff instead of the congressman. In fact, members of congress deal with so many issues on a daily basis, they depend on their staff to tell them who and what to pay attention to. Sometimes you can get in front of the boss on your firsts try, but don't be disappointed if you don't. You'll have a much easier time seeing the congressman in the district than in D.C., mostly because their schedules while at home don't include committee meetings and votes, and they value meeting with constituents. Remember, constituents equal votes.

If your initial meeting is with staff, make sure you show that you value their time and attention to your cause. The better of a job you do convincing them that your information is worth their boss listening to, the more of a chance you'll get that opportunity. It'll be harder to find out information for an ice breaker with a staffer, but you can use the same technique from chapter 8, but you break the ice with their boss through them. You can say something like, "I saw your boss on C-span the other day. Did you help him write that floor speech? I really enjoyed it." Whether they did or didn't help with the speech, they will appreciate that you thought enough of their boss to watch and mention it. Just make sure that a speech was actually made recently, you don't want to get caught in a lie! If your initial meeting is with the lawmaker, use the same format for preparation and execution as described in chapters 7 and 8. If you are meeting about an existing piece of legislation, make sure you know as much as you can about it. The only thing the lawmaker will care about more than what the bill does is who the sponsor and co-sponsors are. If you are trying to get the lawmaker to sponsor a bill for you, they will want you to help them recruit co- sponsors.

Having co-sponsors, and particularly high-profile co-sponsors are currency in congress. You see, there are currently no term limits for congressman. This means that seniority has more to do with the influence of a member as anything else. If a piece of legislation doesn't have co-sponsors who have a powerful committee assignment or a decent amount of seniority, two things that generally go hand-in-hand, then you'll have a hard time moving the bill anywhere. You'll also want to find out what committee or subcommittee the bill has been to or is destined for. Research who sits on those committees, and if the chairman or any of its members have a history of being for or against your issue. You will also have to find out from the committee staff when they expect hearings to be held on the bill. There is also the possibility that a companion bill exists, that is, if a similar bill is being run through the other chamber. Sometimes this tactic is used to expedite the legislative process, as well as give the bill more of a chance for successful passage. If you are working this bill on your own, you'll need to get as much intel as possible as to these key dates so you can plan your travel to D.C. accordingly.

As stated earlier, legislation takes a similar path in congress as it does in state legislatures, but hopefully now you can see that while similar, it's the difference between building a house with Legos and building a skyscraper. Once you get through the long and winding road of the federal legislative process, you still have to get the President of the United States to sign it. Often times, the president is in a different party than the one that controls congress. It's possible that your bill can get delayed for no other reason than a political swordfight between congress and the White House. This is where trade groups, associations, and professional lobbyists can be critical allies. They are used to wading in the murky political waters of Washington, D.C. and can deploy small armies to go out and put pressure on lawmakers to move the legislation along. On your first go around with a federal issue, you can learn a lot from others who have experience at that level. After you have had time to watch and observe the process, you'll slowly build the knowledge and relationships to take on congress by yourself!

Don't be completely discouraged about taking on the 800-pound gorilla by yourself though, after all, you're still new at this. Remember what the prominent American anthropologist Margaret Meade said, "Never doubt that a small group of thoughtful, committed citizens can change the world; indeed, it's the only thing that ever has."

"Democracy is the worst form of government, except for all the others."

-Winston Churchill

CHAPTER ELEVEN

IS THIS REALLY HOW MY GOVERNMENT WORKS?

Unfortunately, this is exactly how your government works. Every election year, some candidate calls for reform and demands that the power be returned to the people instead of to rich corporations and powerful interest groups. The problem is that corporations and interest groups are exactly who funds most of the campaigns around the country.
Do you honestly believe that a candidate would take campaign contributions from these people, and then turn around and vote for reform measures that would diminish their influence on government? If they did, they wouldn't have their jobs for long. The best way to combat this kind of money and power is through grassroots efforts, which is what *Laws and Sausage* hopes to teach everyone who is interested in citizen advocacy.

So, the money pours into Capitol Hill in the form of taxes and campaign contributions, and the sausage comes out in the form of laws, regulations, and of course, pork. "Pork" is a term used to describe the money lawmakers secure for special projects in their districts. This is the most coveted thing in the governing process, because it helps with publicity and re-election. The reality is that the whole system is scripted just like professional wrestling. At the end of the day, Democrat and Republican, Liberal and Conservative, are just ideologies. The only way that the partisan divide really affects the policy process is that it decides who controls the Three branches of government. But no matter who is in charge, the sausage maker works the same way. It just makes different types of sausage depending on which political party is on the crank handle. It's either putting out elephant sausage or donkey sausage, and the average voter usually doesn't have a refined enough pallet to taste the difference.

And after all the time, effort, and money spent on passing laws, they can still be struck down by the signature of a judge. The vision that the founding fathers had for the judiciary was to make sure that the legislative and executive branches didn't overstep their authority. The three branches were actually designed to have checks and balances on each other. The problem we have seen lately in the judiciary is that they are acting like a second legislative branch. Unelected judges with lifetime tenure are creating laws instead of interpreting them. In fact, a common strategy for activism is to shop around for judges who lean a certain way politically in order to get an injunction for laws passed by elected representatives, and sometimes approved by a referendum of the voters. There can be an entire book written about judicial activism, but for the purposes of this book, just be aware that after the grueling sausage making process, the third branch of government is lurking in the shadows and can easily reverse all of your hard work.

As stated earlier in this book, on average, it takes many attempts to pass legislation before the effort is successful. Don't be discouraged if your bill gets derailed somewhere along its way through the sausage maker, you've gained valuable experience and created many important relationships. The first thing you'll want to do (besides take a breather, or maybe a vacation!), is make a list of everything that went right and wrong. Every meeting that went well, the ones that didn't go so well, which committees your legislation passed, what type of questions were asked, and of course, where it finally failed. This will be your blueprint for the next go around. The second thing you should do is draft letters to every policy maker you met with in the process. This can be done via e-mail, and it is important to copy the staffer who was the most helpful to you on the correspondence.

If somewhere in the process a lawmaker decided not to support you, withdrew support, or changed their vote without telling you, it's important not to get emotional. Politics is a moving target; most lawmakers make decisions by sticking their thumbs in the air to see which way the political wind is blowing. The next time you take a swing at influencing the public policy process, you may find that you have new allies as well as new opponents. Don't forget, the two main components of politics are perception and misdirection. Relationships and credibility, however, are currency. The two most unforgivable sins in politics are lying and burning bridges.

You will no doubt deal with the same policy makers again on your subsequent attempts to promote your cause, so there is absolutely no benefit in getting sideways with someone just because they weren't on your side. Conversely, don't assume that an ally on the last campaign will automatically be with you on the next one. They may still be in favor of your cause, but if they believe that the political environment hasn't evolved enough to give your bill a much better chance of passing, they may pass on it themselves. You see, lawmakers lose a little bit of political capital every time one of their bills fail. It is unlikely that they will be willing to carry it again if they think it will fail again. For a refresher, go back and re-read chapter 6 for advice on proper political timing. Either way, you will want everyone you encountered during the process to remember you as professional and well-informed. This will increase the likelihood that they will be willing to work with you again. You never know what side the policy makers will be on the next time you step up to the plate, so you don't want to give anyone a reason to blow you off. Again, it all depends on the political winds, so don't leave a tornado in your wake.

The success of your campaign is dependent on many factors, but two of the most important will be the level of government you are starting at, and how controversial your cause is, if at all. If your target venue of jurisdiction is local, and your issue is not considered "hot button", you may have success on your first try. But the sausage maker cranks slowly, so the reality is that it will probably take a while. But whether you hit a home run your first time up, or you finally succeed after a few tries, you will need to be careful how you deal with the aftermath. Of course, there is call for celebration, you've worked hard and earned night out on the town (assuming that is your thing). But victory laps can be a tricky thing. I'm not suggesting you run around the building high-fiving lawmakers, but it can be advantageous for you to build on your new political capital.

The first thing you should do is, much like if you were unsuccessful, is draft letters of thanks to all the policy makers who supported you, also via e-mail while copying the point staffer who you had the most communication with. It is not necessary to send correspondence to the policy makers who were not with you, mostly because it could be interpreted as rubbing the victory in their faces. The feelings of elected officials can be very delicate, so it's better to not risk offending them even if your intentions are noble. The reason why I suggest e-mail is because postal mail, in many cases, can be screened by security depending on the level of government the policy maker serves in. This can slow down the delivery process as well as increase the chances of the letter being lost. I also don't suggest that you type your letter in the body of the e-mail. Staffers read the majority of incoming e-mails and then decide which ones they will pass along to their boss.

Most lawmakers get so many e-mails that staffers might skip some if they don't appear urgent enough. You should type a professional letter, properly formatted and on your letterhead, and send it as an attachment in the e-mail. In the subject line, put something like "(Lawmaker's name and title) – EYES ONLY". This will definitely get attention because the staffer will assume that nobody but their boss should open it, so natural human curiosity will make it hard to pass up. In the body of the e-mail, simply write "Please see attached." This gives no indication of what the letter says, so it greatly increases the chance that it will be opened. In your letter, in addition to thanking the lawmaker, you also will want to mention by name the staffers who were helpful to you. Since it will make the staffer look good in front of their boss, you can bet a dollar to a donut that he or she will print the letter and make sure that the lawmaker reads it.

There is nothing unethical or manipulative about these techniques, you are simply using the human condition to predict the best outcome for your efforts.

In chapter 5, we talked about how to create awareness for your campaign. Now that you have used all the techniques in this books to successfully effectuate change, it is important to create a little post-publicity for yourself. The best way to do this is to send out a press release. There is an example of a draft press release in the "Resources" section of this book. Most media outlets in your area will have a fax number or e-mail address to their news rooms listed on their websites. The more copies you send out, the better chance you will have of your release being published. They may just print your release as written or paraphrase it, but there is also a chance that a reporter will contact you for a comment. It's important not to make the interview all about you, but rather stick to the basic talking points in your elevator pitch. If possible, mention the name of the lawmaker(s) who sponsored your legislation, they will appreciate the free publicity.

Relationships with the media can be just as beneficial as those with policy makers. At the same time, it is also important to guard your credibility with the media. You don't want to get on the wrong side of a person who buys ink by the tanker and paper by the truckload. But the right kind of publicity can help you become well known your area of expertise, and can make you more successful in your future endeavors.

You now have learned just enough about the policy making process to be dangerous. Hopefully, this book will serve as a guide to be referred to each time you decide to take up a new cause. Many of the tips and tricks contained herein can be duplicated, therefore I hope that it will become a valued reference in your library. There will be ups and downs, good days and bad, and victories and defeats. The more times you go through the process, the better you will become at it. If you ever become nervous or intimidated by the sausage making just because you are still an amateur, just remember this: Noah's ark was built by amateurs, the Titanic was built by professionals. Happy hunting!

If you belong to an organization that would like to have Brian Trascher speak at your next conference or corporate meeting, or if your organization would be interested in more advanced advocacy training, Laws and Sausage offers keynote address services as well as a one-day workshop that can be presented on-site. Please visit www.lawsandsausage.net for more information.

RESOURCES

APPENDIX A: THE FOLLOW UP LETTER

The Honorable (Title & Name)
Address

Dear (Title and Name):

I wanted to take the opportunity to thank you and your staff for making the time to meet with my team and I regarding (your issue). I also appreciate your willingness to sponsor legislation on our behalf, as well as your support throughout the process.

Additionally, I wanted you to know how much I appreciated the help of (key staffer) in coordinating our meetings as well as keeping us all up to date with our progress. If we can ever be of service to you or your office, please don't hesitate to contact me.

Sincerely,

(Your name)
(Name of Group or Organization)

APPENDIX B: THE PRESS RELEASE

(Date)
FOR IMMEDIATE RELEASE
CONTACT: (Your Name and Phone Number)

(Headline: Announce the final result of law passage or most significant action of your campaign. Either underline or use all caps.)

(City: Either your home town or where the most action of your campaign took place) – Today Governor (Name) signed in to law HB123 which (Purpose of your legislation). The bill was authored by (Legislator) and co-authored by (Legislators). (Encourage the author to make a comment, then insert it here.)

The measure was filed at the request of (Your organization), a group who has been promoting (Your cause) since (when your campaign started). (Add your own comment here, include your title or role in the organization if applicable).

The law goes into effect on (Date).

-30-
(-30- is just media-speak for "the end")

APPENDIX C: U.S. STATE WEBSITES

www.alabama.gov
www.alaska.gov
www.az.gov
www.arkansas.gov
www.ca.gov
www.colorado.gov
www.ct.gov
www.delaware.gov
www.myflorida.com
www.georgia.gov
www.ehawaii.gov
www.idaho.gov
www.illinois.gov
www.in.gov
www.iowa.gov
www.kansas.gov
www.kentucky.gov
www.louisiana.gov
www.maine.gov
www.maryland.gov
www.mass.gov
www.michigan.gov
www.state.mn.us
www.ms.gov
www.mo.gov

www.mt.gov
www.nebraska.gov
www.nv.gov
www.nh.gov
www.nj.gov
www.newmexico.gov
www.ny.gov
www.ncgov.gov
www.nd.com
www.ohio.gov
www.ok.gov
www.oregon.gov
www.pa.gov
www.ri.gov
www.sc.gov
www.sd.gov
www.tennessee.gov
www.texasonline.gov
www.utah.gov
www.vermont.gov
www.virginia.gov
www.wa.gov
www.wv.us
www.wisconsin.gov
www.wyoming.gov

APPENDIX D: U.S. GOVERNMENT WEBSITES

U.S. House of Representatives:

www.house.gov

U.S. Senate:

www.senate.gov

President of the United States:

www.whitehouse.gov

U.S. Constitution

https://www.whitehouse.gov/1600/constitution

List of U.S. Government Agencies:

https://www.usa.gov/federal-agencies/a

Comprehensive search engine for all U.S. Government websites:

www.USA.gov

INDEX

A
Abramoff Lobbying Scandal, 11
American Legislative Process, viii

B
Bad Lobbyists, 2
Baton Rouge Metro Council, 45
Benefits of Having a Group, 18
Bicameral Legislature, 73
Bicameral Legislatures, 27
Biggest Donors, 23
Bill Clinton's Staff, xvi
Body of Jurisdiction, 6
Bully Pulpit, 29
Bush, George H.W., xv

C
Campaign Donations Benefit, 24
Carter, Jimmy, xiii
Caucuses, 30
City Council Member, 23, 25, 44, 49
Clinton, Bill, xv-xvi
Co-Sponsors, 30, 81-82
Committee Structure, 27
Community Educators, 13
Conference Committee, 77
Conference Report, 77-78
Congressional Level, x
Congressional Staff, 80

D
Democracy, ix, 63, 85

E
Editor's Contact Info, 20
Effective Technique, 19, 37
Eight hundred Pound Gorilla, 28, 83
Elevator Pitch, 51-52, 56-59, 61, 66, 72, 92
Evolutionary Chart, 16
Executive Level, 27
  Agriculture, 28

INDEX

Budgetary and Fiscal Matters, 28
Criminal Law, 28
Education, 28, 30
Environment, 28, 89
Healthcare, 28, 30
Insurance, 28
Labor, 28, 31, 58
Land and Mineral Rights, 28
State Constitution, 28, 75
Transportation and Infrastructure, 28, 30

F
Facebook, 35-37
Federal Level, 10, 52, 66, 79-80

G
Government Works, 85-86
Governmental Relations Professionals, 2, 11
Group of Lobbyists, 11
Gulf South Strategies, xvii

H
High-Fiving Lawmakers, 90

High-Profile Co-Sponsors, 81
High-Rise Office Tower, 26
Higher Chamber, 27
House Appropriations Committee, xiv
House Districts, 27
House of Representatives, 23, 27, 99

I
Information About Non-Profits, 18
Initial Meeting, 42, 80-81
Internal Revenue Service, 9
Interstate Highway System, 2

J
Judicial Activism, 87
Judiciary, 31, 87
Jurisdiction of the Federal Government, 30

L
Lawmaker's Language, 56
Lawmakers, 65, 80, 83, 86, 88-91
Legislation, ix-x, 5-6, 8-9, 16, 45, 49, 52, 58, 71, 79, 81-83, 88, 92,

INDEX

96-97
Legislative Branch, 2,
  25-26, 29, 31, 71, 87
Legitimate Governmental
  Relations
  Professionals, 11
Livingston, Bob, xiv
Lobbyist Activities, 11
Lobbyist Disclosure Act,
  10
Lobbyists, x, xvii, 1-2,
  11, 13, 16, 79, 83
Local Issues, 25
Louisiana State
  University, xv

M
Meade, Margaret, 83
Motor Voter Law, 4
Municipal Government,
  26
  Drainage Issues, 26
  Infrastructure
    Maintenance, 26
  Local Public Safety,
    26
  Occupational
    Licenses, 26
  Rent Laws, 26
  Zoning, 26

N
New Orleans Politics, 42
Non-Controversial Bill,
  75
Non-Profit Organizations,
  13, 18
Nusslein, Rick, xiv

O
O'Neil, Tip, 22-23

P
Paramount in Politics, 19
Partisan Gridlock, x
Petition the Government,
  9
Planning and Zoning, 26
Policy Maker, 4, 6, 9,
  11-13, 16-17, 24, 49,
  51, 56-58, 60-61,
  67-68, 71, 88-92
Policy Making Process,
  15, 93
Political Campaigns, xiii
Political Environment, 89
Political Game, 5, 19
Political Temperature, 6
Pop-in, 51
Preparing Public
  Testimony, 6
Public Policy Process,
  ix-x, 18, 24, 88
Public Testimony, 6, 72,
  74

INDEX

R
Reagan, Ronald, xiii
Reagan-Carter Debate, xiii
Registered Voters, 23
Republican National Convention, xv

S
Saxe, John Godfrey, viii
Seasoned Lobbyist, 2 Second Oldest
   Profession, viii, 16
Senate Activities, 76
Senate Districts, 27
Supreme Court, 31

T
Targeting Key Staffers, 6
Taxpayer Advocacy Program, 9
Timing of My Campaign, 41
Trascher, Brian, xi, 93
Twitter, 35, 37-38

U
U.S Congress, x, 29, 78
U.S House of Representatives, 23
U.S Senator, 9, 25
Unintended Consequences, 4-5

W
Wordpress, 38-39

Made in the USA
Middletown, DE
04 May 2017